Deep Thoughts

by
Jack Handey

BERKLEY BOOKS, NEW YORK

DEEP THOUGHTS

A Berkley Book / published by arrangement with
the author

PRINTING HISTORY
Berkley trade paperback edition / June 1992

ISBN: 0-425-13365-6

A BERKLEY BOOK ® TM 757,375
Berkley Books are published by The Berkley Publishing Group,
200 Madison Avenue, New York, New York 10016.
The name "BERKLEY" and the "B" logo
are trademarks belonging to Berkley Publishing Corporation.

PRINTED IN THE UNITED STATES OF AMERICA

30 29 28 27 26 25 24 23

To Marta

Special thanks to:

George Meyer, John Fortenberry, Tom Gammill,
Max Pross, Fred Graver,
Ed Wintermantel, Lorne Michaels,
Byron Laursen, Chris Hart, William Novak,
Michael Nesmith and, most especially,
Marta Chavez Handey.

It takes a big man to cry,
but it takes a bigger man
to laugh at that man.

_____

If you ever fall off the Sears Tower, just go real limp, because maybe you'll look like a dummy and people will try to catch you because, hey, free dummy.

If a kid asks where rain comes from, I think a cute thing to tell him is "God is crying." And if he asks why God is crying, another cute thing to tell him is "Probably because of something you did."

To me, boxing is like a ballet, except there's no music, no choreography, and the dancers hit each other.

If trees could scream, would we be so cavalier about cutting them down? We might, if they screamed all the time, for no good reason.

Better not take a dog on the Space Shuttle, because if he sticks his head out when you're coming home his face might burn up.

To me, clowns aren't funny. In fact, they're kinda scary. I've wondered where this started, and I think it goes back to the time I went to the circus and a clown killed my dad.

I'd like to see a nude opera, because when they hit those high notes I bet you can really see it in those genitals.

C ontrary to popular belief, the most dangerous animal is not the lion or tiger or even the elephant. The most dangerous animal is a shark riding on an elephant, just trampling and eating everything they see.

As we were driving, we saw a sign that said "Watch For Rocks." Marta said it should read "Watch For _Pretty_ Rocks." I told her she should write in her suggestion to the highway department, but she started saying it was a joke—just to get out of writing a simple letter! And I thought I was lazy!

As I bit into the nectarine, it had a crisp juiciness about it that was very pleasurable—until I realized it wasn't a nectarine at all, but A HUMAN HEAD!!

*O*nce, when I was in Hawaii, on the island of Kauai, I met a mysterious old stranger. He said he was about to die and wanted to tell someone about the treasure. I said, "Okay, as long as it's not a long story. Some of us have a plane to catch, you know."

He started telling his story, about the treasure and his life and all, and I thought: "This story isn't too long." But then, he kept going, and I started thinking, "Uh-oh, this story is getting long." But then, the story was over, and I said to myself: "You know, that story wasn't too long after all."

I forget what the story was about, but there was a good movie on the plane. It was a little long, though.

If you ever teach a yodeling class, probably the hardest thing is to keep the students from just trying to yodel right off. You see, we <u>build</u> to that.

Is there anything more beautiful than a beautiful, beautiful flamingo, flying across in front of a beautiful sunset? And he's carrying a beautiful rose in his beak, and also he's carrying a very beautiful painting with his feet. And also, you're drunk.

I guess of all my uncles, I liked Uncle Cave Man the best. We called him Uncle Cave Man because he lived in a cave and because sometimes he'd eat one of us. Later on we found out he was a bear.

Anytime I see something screech across a room and latch onto someone's neck, and the guy screams and tries to get it off, I have to laugh, because what _is_ that thing?!

In weightlifting, I don't think sudden, uncontrolled urination should automatically disqualify you.

If you're a horse, and someone gets on you, and falls off, and then gets right back on you, I think you should buck him off right away.

*I f you define cowardice
as running away at the
first sign of danger,
screaming and tripping
and begging for mercy,
then yes, Mister Brave Man,
I guess I am a coward.*

The memories of my family outings are still a source of strength to me. I remember we'd all pile into the car—I forget what kind it was—and drive and drive. I'm not sure where we'd go, but I think there were some trees there. The smell of something was strong in the air as we played whatever sport we played. I remember a bigger, older guy we called "Dad." We'd eat some stuff, or not, and then I think we went home.

I guess some things never leave you.

Blow ye winds,
Like the trumpet blows;
But without that noise.

I *wish a robot would get elected President. That way, when he came to town, we could all take a shot at him and not feel too bad.*

He was a cowboy, mister, and he loved the land. He loved it so much he made a woman out of dirt and married her. But when he kissed her, she disintegrated. Later, at the funeral, when the preacher said "Dust to dust," some people laughed, and the cowboy shot them. At his hanging, he told the others, "I'll be waiting for you in heaven—with a gun."

When the age of the Vikings came to a close, they must have sensed it. Probably, they gathered together one evening, slapped each other on the back and said, "Hey, good job."

If you go parachuting, and your parachute doesn't open, and your friends are all watching you fall, I think a funny gag would be to pretend you were swimming.

Sometimes when I feel like killing someone, I do a little trick to calm myself down. I'll go over to the person's house and ring the doorbell. When the person comes to the door, I'm gone, but you know what I've left on the porch? A jack-o'-lantern with a knife in the side of its head with a note that says "You."

After that, I usually feel a lot better, and no harm done.

I can still recall old Mister Barnslow getting out every morning and nailing a fresh load of tadpoles to that old board of his. Then he'd spin it round and round, like a wheel of fortune, and no matter where it stopped he'd yell out, "Tadpoles! Tadpoles is a winner!"

We all thought he was crazy. But then, we had some growing up to do.

The face of a child can say
it all, especially the
mouth part of the face.

_____

If I ever opened a trampoline store, I don't think I'd call it Trampo-Land, because you might think it was a store for tramps, which is not the impression we are trying to convey with our store. On the other hand, we would not prohibit tramps from browsing, or testing the trampolines, unless a tramp's gyrations seemed to be getting out of control.

I wish I had a kryptonite cross, because then you could keep both Dracula _and_ Superman away.

Too bad you can't just grab a tree by the very tiptop and bend it clear over the ground and then let her fly, because I bet you'd be amazed at all the stuff that comes flying out.

I remember that fateful day when Coach took me aside. I knew what was coming. "You don't have to tell me," I said. "I'm off the team, aren't I?"

"Well," said Coach, "you never were really <u>on</u> the team. You made that uniform you're wearing out of rags and towels, and your helmet is a toy space helmet. You show up at practice and then either steal the ball and make us chase you to get it back, or you try to tackle people at inappropriate times."

It was all true what he was saying. And yet, I thought, something is brewing inside the head of this Coach. He sees something in me, some kind of raw talent that he can mold. But that's when I felt the handcuffs go on.

If you saw two guys named Hambone and Flippy, which one would you think liked dolphins the most? I'd say Flippy, wouldn't you? You'd be wrong though. It's Hambone.

When I heard that trees grow a new "ring" for each year they live, I thought, we humans are kind of like that: we grow a new layer of skin each year, and after many years we are thick and unwieldy from all our skin layers.

L aurie got offended
that I used the word
"puke." But to me,
that's what her dinner
tasted like.

If you're in a boxing match, try not to let the other guy's glove touch your lips, because you don't know where that glove has been.

_____

I t's too bad that whole
families have to be
torn apart by some-
thing as simple as wild
dogs.

Marta says the interesting thing about fly fishing is that it's two lives connected by a thin strand. Come on, Marta. Grow up.

The old pool shooter had won many a game in his life. But now it was time to hang up the cue. When he did, all the other cues came crashing to the floor.

"Sorry," he said with a smile.

I f I ever do a book on the Amazon, I hope I am able to bring a certain lightheartedness to the subject, in a way that tells the reader we are going to have fun with this thing.

Even though he was an enemy of mine, I had to admit that what he had accomplished was a brilliant piece of strategy. First, he punched me, then he kicked me, then he punched me again.

If you're at a Thanks-giving dinner, but you don't like the stuffing or the cranberry sauce or anything else, just pretend like you're eating it, but instead, put it all in your lap and form it into a big mushy ball. Then, later, when you're out back having cigars with the boys, let out a big fake cough and throw the ball to the ground. Then say, "Boy, these are good cigars!"

M ost people don't realize that large pieces of coral, which have been painted brown and attached to the skull by common wood screws, can make a child look like a deer.

The sound of fresh rain run-off splashing from the roof reminded me of the sound of urine splashing into a filthy Texaco latrine.

I think somebody should come up with a way to breed a very large shrimp. That way, you could ride him, then, after you camped at night, you could eat him.

How about it, science?

When you go for a job interview, I think a good thing to ask is if they ever press charges.

I bet the main reason the police keep people away from a plane crash is they don't want anybody walking in and lying down in the crash stuff, then when somebody comes up act like they just woke up and go, "What was <u>that</u>?!"

I scrambled to the top of the precipice where Nick was waiting.

"That was fun," I said.

"You bet it was," said Nick. "Let's climb higher."

"No," I said. "I think we should be heading back now."

"We have time," Nick insisted.

I said we didn't, and Nick said we did. We argued back and forth like that for about 20 minutes, then finally decided to head back.

I didn't say it was an interesting story.

If you're a young Mafia gangster out on your first date, I bet it's really embarrassing if someone tries to kill you.

*S*ome folks say it was a miracle. Saint Francis suddenly appeared and knocked the next pitch clean over the fence. But I think it was just a lucky swing.

Too bad there's not such a thing as a <u>golden</u> skunk, because you'd probably be <u>proud</u> to be sprayed by one.

I bet one legend that keeps recurring throughout history, in every culture, is the story of Popeye.

To me, truth is not some vague, foggy notion. Truth is real. And, at the same time, unreal. Fiction and fact and everything in between, plus some things I can't remember, all rolled into one big "thing." This is truth, to me.

Whenever I see an old lady slip and fall on a wet sidewalk, my first instinct is to laugh. But then I think, what if I was an ant, and she fell on me. Then it wouldn't seem quite so funny.

Y*ou know what would make a good story? Something about a clown who makes people happy, but inside he's real sad. Also, he has severe diarrhea.*

I bet a fun thing would be to go way back in time to where there was going to be an eclipse and tell the cave men, "If I have come to destroy you, may the sun be blotted out from the sky." Just then the eclipse would start, and they'd probably try to kill you or something, but then you could explain about the rotation of the moon and all, and everyone would get a good laugh.

We used to laugh at Grandpa when he'd head off to go fishing. But we wouldn't be laughing that evening, when he'd come back with some whore he picked up in town.

I think in one of my
previous lives I was a
mighty king, because I
like people to do what I
say.

T oday I accidentally stepped on a snail on the sidewalk in front of our house. And I thought, I too am like that snail. I build a defensive wall around myself, a "shell" if you will. But my shell isn't made out of a hard, protective substance. Mine is made out of tinfoil and paper bags.

A man doesn't automatically get my respect. He has to get down in the dirt and beg for it.

One thing kids like is to be tricked. For instance, I was going to take my little nephew to Disneyland, but instead I drove him to an old burned-out warehouse. "Oh, no," I said, "Disneyland burned down."

He cried and cried, but I think that deep down, he thought it was a pretty good joke.

I started to drive over to the real Disneyland, but it was getting pretty late.

As the evening sun faded from a salmon color to a sort of flint gray, I thought back to the salmon I caught that morning, and how gray he was, and how I named him Flint.

If you're ever stuck in some thick under-growth, in your under-wear, don't stop and start thinking of what other words have "under" in them, because that's probably the first sign of jungle madness.

S ometimes the beauty of the world is so overwhelming, I just want to throw back my head and gargle. Just gargle and gargle, and I don't care who hears me, because I am beautiful.

Fear can sometimes be a useful emotion. ~~For instance, let's~~ say you're an astronaut on the moon and you fear that your partner has been turned into Dracula. The next time he goes out for the moon pieces, wham!, you just slam the door behind him and blast off. He might call you on the radio and say he's not Dracula, but you just say, "Think again, bat man."

I wish scientists would come up with a way to make dogs a lot bigger, but with a smaller head. That way, they'd still be good as watchdogs, but they wouldn't eat so much.

I bet for an Indian, shooting an old fat pioneer woman in the back with an arrow, and she fires her shotgun into the ground as she falls over, is like the top thing you can do.

I think a good movie
would be about a guy
who's a brain scientist,
but he gets hit on the head
and it damages the part of
the brain that makes you
want to study the brain.

I *wouldn't be surprised if someday some fishermen caught a big shark and cut it open, and there inside was a whole person. Then they cut the person open, and in him is a little baby shark. And in the baby shark there isn't a person, because it would be too small. But there's a little doll or something, like a Johnny Combat little toy guy—something like that.*

It makes me mad when I go to all the trouble of having Marta cook up about a hundred drumsticks, then the guy at Marineland says, "You can't throw chicken to the dolphins. They eat fish."

Sure they eat fish, if that's all you give them. Man, wise up.

If the Vikings were around today, they would probably be amazed at how much glow-in-the-dark stuff we have, and how we take so much of it for granted.

We tend to scoff at
the beliefs of the
ancients. But we
can't scoff at them person-
ally, to their faces, and
this is what annoys me.

It's not good to let any kid near a container that has a skull and crossbones on it, because there might be a skeleton costume inside and the kid could put it on and really scare you.

If you had a school for professional fireworks people, I don't think you could cover fuses in just one class. It's just too rich a subject.

People think it would be fun to be a bird because you could fly. But they forget the negative side, which is the preening.

_____

If I lived back in the Wild West days, instead of carrying a six-gun in my holster, I'd carry a soldering iron. That way, if some smart-aleck cowboy said something like "Hey, look. He's carrying a soldering iron!" and started laughing, and everybody else started laughing, I could just say, "That's right, it's a soldering iron. The soldering iron of justice."

Then everybody would get real quiet and ashamed, because they made fun of the soldering iron of justice, and I could probably hit them up for a free drink.

When I think back on all the blessings I have been given in my life, I can't think of a single one, unless you count that rattlesnake that granted me all those wishes.

I hope in the future Americans are thought of as a warlike, vicious people, because I bet a lot of high schools would pick "Americans" as their mascot.

Sometimes I think the world has gone completely mad. And then I think, "Aw, who cares?" And then I think, "Hey, what's for supper?"

_____

If you ever discover that
what you're seeing is a
play within a play, just
slow down, take a deep
breath, and hold on for
the ride of your life.

I can see why it would be prohibited to throw most things off the top of the Empire State Building, but what's wrong with little bits of cheese? They probably break down into their various gases before they even hit.

I f you're a circus clown, and you have a dog that you use in your act, I don't think it's a good idea to also dress the dog up like a clown, because people see that and they think, "Forgive me, but that's just too *much*."

H ere's a good joke to do during an earth-quake: straddle a big crack in the ground, and if it opens wider, go "Whoa! Whoa!" and flail your arms around, like you're going to fall in.

*I*f you ever go tempo-
rarily insane, don't
shoot somebody, like a
lot of people do. Instead,
try to get some weeding
done, because you'd really
be surprised.

I t makes me mad when people say I turned and ran like a scared rabbit. Maybe it was like an angry rabbit, who was running to go fight in another fight, away from the first fight.

I hope if dogs ever take over the world, and they choose a king, they don't just go by size, because I bet there are some Chihuahuas with some good ideas.

I *think a good way to
get into a movie is to
show up where they're
making the movie, then
stick a big cactus plant
onto your buttocks and
start yowling and running
around. Everyone would
think it was funny, and
the head movie guy would
say, "Hey, let's put him in
the movie."*

*W*hat is it that
makes a complete
stranger dive into
an icy river to save a solid
gold baby? Maybe we'll
never know.

*I*nstead of having "answers" on a math test, they should just call them "impressions," and if you got a different "impression," so what, can't we all be brothers?

If God dwells inside us, like some people say, I sure hope He likes enchiladas, because that's what He's getting!

Probably to a shark, about the funniest thing there is is a wounded seal, trying to swim to shore, because where does he think he's going?!

Perhaps, if I am very lucky, the feeble efforts of my lifetime will someday be noticed, and maybe, in some small way, they will be acknowledged as the greatest works of genius ever created by Man.